# Contents

Grim Greeks. . . . . . . . . . . . . . . . . . . . . 4

Who were the Ancient Greeks? . . . . 6

Becoming a Greek warrior . . . . . . . . 8

Fighting wars . . . . . . . . . . . . . . . . . 12

Greek weapons. . . . . . . . . . . . . . . . 18

Famous Greek warriors . . . . . . . . . . 22

Greek women . . . . . . . . . . . . . . . . . 24

Greeks versus Romans . . . . . . . . . . 26

Greek warrior activity . . . . . . . . . . . 28

Glossary. . . . . . . . . . . . . . . . . . . . . 30

Find out more . . . . . . . . . . . . . . . . . 31

Index . . . . . . . . . . . . . . . . . . . . . . . 32

# Grim Greeks

Place: Greece
Date: 431 BC

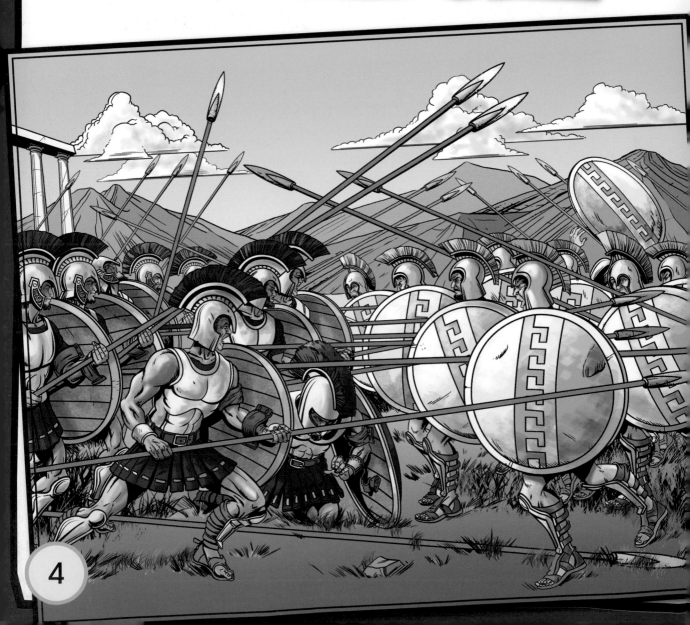

4

# Fierce Fighters
# GREEK
# ...ORS

## Charlotte Guillain

**www.raintreepublishers.co.uk**
Visit our website to find out more information about Raintree books.

**To order:**

☎ Phone 0845 6044371
📄 Fax +44 (0) 1865 312263
💻 Email myorders@raintreepublishers.co.uk

Customers from outside the UK please telephone +44 1865 312262

Raintree is an imprint of Capstone Global Library Limited, a company incorporated in England and Wales having its registered office at 7 Pilgrim Street, London, EC4V 6LB – Registered company number: 6695582

Edited by Rebecca Rissman, Nancy Dickmann, and Catherine Veitch
Designed by Joanna Hinton-Malivoire
Picture research by Tracy Cummins
Original illlustrations © Capstone Global Library 2010
Original illustrations by Miracle Studios
Production by Victoria Fitzgerald
Originated by Capstone Global Library
Printed and bound in China by Leo Paper Products

ISBN 978 1 406 21615 8 (hardback)
14 13 12 11 10
10 9 8 7 6 5 4 3 2 1

ISBN 978 1 406 21709 4 (paperback)
15 14 13 12 11
10 9 8 7 6 5 4 3 2 1

**British Library Cataloguing in Publication Data**
Guillain, Charlotte.
Greek warriors. -- (Fierce fighters)
355.1'0938-dc22

**Acknowledgements**
We would like to thank the following for permission to reproduce photographs: Alamy pp. **9** (© Photos 12), **17** (© Peter Horree), **24** (© North Wind Picture Archives), **25** (© The London Art Archive); Art Resource, NY pp. **13** (Réunion des Musées Nationaux), **18** (Erich Lessing); Corbis pp. **11** (© René Mattes/Hemis), **26** (© Charles & Josette Lenars), **7** (©Dallas and John Heaton); Getty Images pp. **10** (Penelope Painter), **23** (Charles Le Brun); Heinemann Raintree pp. **28** (Karon Dubke), **29 top** (Karon Dubke), **29 bottom** (Karon Dubke); Shutterstock p. **19** (© bkp); The Art Archive pp. **12** (Archaeological Museum Ferrara / Alfredo Dagli Orti), **14** (Museo di Villa Giulia Rome / Gianni Dagli Orti), **22** (Staatliche Glypothek Munich / Alfredo Dagli Orti); The Granger Collection, New York p. **27**.

Front cover photograph of a Greek battle reproduced with permission of Miracle Studios.

The publishers would like to thank Jane Penrose for her assistance in the preparation of this book.

Every effort has been made to contact copyright holders of material reproduced in this book. Any omissions will be rectified in subsequent printings if notice is given to the publishers.

All the internet addresses (URLs) given in this book were valid at the time of going to press. However, due to the dynamic nature of the Internet, some addresses may have changed or ceased to exist since publication. While the author and publishers regret any inconvenience this may cause readers, no responsibility for any such changes can be accepted by either the author or the publishers.

Some words are shown in bold, **like this**. You can find out what they mean by looking in the glossary.

Two armies are marching towards each other. Suddenly the enemies smash into each other. Swords and **spears** clash. **Warriors** roar. Dying soldiers scream.

The Greek armies are at war again!

## Greek timeline

| | |
|---|---|
| **776 BC** | First Olympic Games in Greece |
| **460-340 BC** | Many battles between Sparta and other Greek city-states |
| **146 BC** | Rome conquers Greece |
| **AD 1400s** | Columbus sails to America |
| **1600s** | People from Europe start to settle in North America |
| **2000s** | You are reading this book |

# Who were the Ancient Greeks?

Ancient Greece was made up of different cities and the land around them, called **city-states**. Each city-state had a ruler. These rulers often fought each other to get more land and become more powerful.

## The Ancient Greek Empire

Key

■ Ancient Greek Empire
— country border today

This statue shows Perseus, a warrior from Ancient Greek stories. Perseus cut off the head of a monster called Medusa.

# Becoming a Greek warrior

In Athens young Greek men had to train as soldiers for two years. They had to buy their own **armour** and weapons. After two years they finished training and only had to fight if their ruler started a war.

We can learn about Ancient Greek heroes from films.

In Sparta all boys started training as soldiers when they were seven years old. They did a lot of sport and practised using their weapons. Groups of boys had to fight each other so they would become mean and **violent**.

This jar shows two boys learning to fight.

## DID YOU KNOW?

Twelve-year-old Spartan boys had to wear the same thin **tunic** all year round to make them tough.

# Fighting wars

When a ruler went to war, all men would fight in the army. They wanted to **protect** their homes and families. Soldiers in the same army painted their shields with the same colours. Then they knew who the enemy was as they fought.

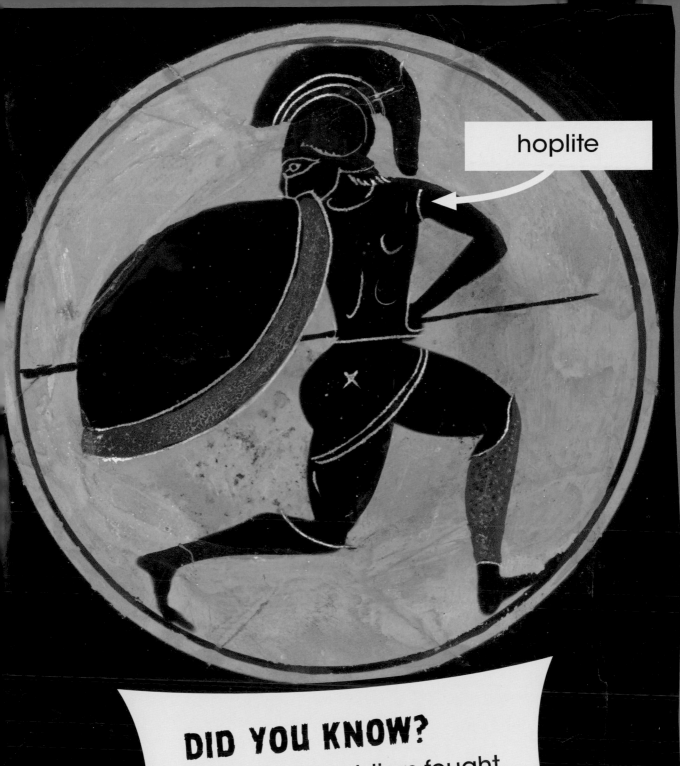

hoplite

## DID YOU KNOW?

Most Greek soldiers fought on foot. They were called *hoplites* (say *hop-light*).

Foot soldiers had to be very fit and skilled. But they also had to work as a team. They ran at the enemy in a tight rectangle, called a **phalanx** [say *fa-lanks*]. They held up their shields together and stuck out their **spears**.

## DID YOU KNOW?

When the soldiers in a phalanx held up their shields they overlapped. This made it hard for the enemy to attack.

Some **city-states** had special soldiers who fought on their own. They ran at the enemy, throwing **spears** and breaking up the **phalanxes**.

## DID YOU KNOW?

Other soldiers galloped into battle on horses. This was a scary sight for the foot soldiers.

# Greek weapons

Most of the soldiers in a Greek army wore **armour** and metal helmets and carried a wooden shield. Most foot soldiers carried a long spear called a **dory** and a sword. Some Greek warriors also used bows and arrows.

bow and arrow

Other soldiers were stone-slingers. They used a special **sling** to throw stones into battle. The stones could hit their enemies on the head. But sometimes they also hit their own army!

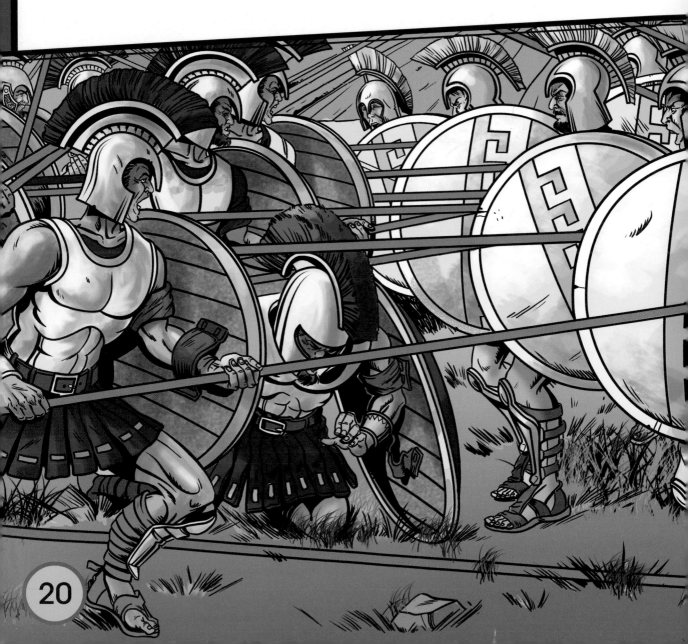

sling

## DID YOU KNOW?

Some soldiers trained to throw stones by hand, without a sling.

21

Alexander the Great was a king in the north of Greece. Alexander was a strong leader who knew how to beat his enemies and win a war.

22

Alexander the Great

## DID YOU KNOW?

Alexander built many new cities and often called them "Alexandria" after himself!

# Greek women

Most Greek women had to stay at home and look after children. But in Sparta things were different. Spartan women ran in races, wrestled, and could play sports. They brought up their children to learn how to fight.

Spartan girl

## DID YOU KNOW?

Ancient Greek stories told of warrior women called the Amazons. They were ruled by a queen and kept men as **slaves**.

# Greeks versus Romans

In the end, the Roman army beat the Greek **warriors**. The Romans took over all the Greek lands and became the most powerful rulers in the world. The days of Greek warriors were over.

Roman soldiers

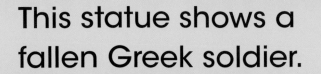

This statue shows a
fallen Greek soldier.

Greek soldiers ate sesame seeds to give them energy as they marched into battle.

## Make your own sesame buns

**You will need:**

- 500g whole wheat flour
- 250 ml milk
- 125 ml olive oil
- 3 eggs
- 1 teaspoon salt
- 200g sesame seeds
- 250 ml honey
- a greased baking tray

1. Preheat the oven to 180°C (356°F).

2. Mix the salt with the flour and add the olive oil and eggs. **Knead** the mixture.

3. Add the milk, half the honey, and half the sesame seeds.

 **Always have an adult with you when you are cooking.**

**4.** Form the mixture into bun shapes. Put them on the baking tray.

**5.** Make a small hole in the middle of each bun. Fill the holes with the rest of the honey. Sprinkle the rest of the sesame seeds over the buns.

**6.** Bake for 40 minutes, until they are golden brown.

# Glossary

**armour** leather or metal covering to protect a solider

**city-state** area made up of a city and the land and villages around it. Each city-state had its own ruler.

**dory** a long, light spear used as a weapon by Greek warriors

**knead** press down dough with hands

**phalanx** group of soldiers moving closely together into battle

**protect** keep from getting hurt

**slave** person who is owned by someone else. Slaves had to work hard and didn't get paid.

**sling** strap used to throw a stone as a weapon

**spear** weapon with sharp blade on a long pole

**tunic** loose piece of clothing with no sleeves

**violent** behaving in a rough way that will hurt others

**warrior** fighter

# Find out more

## Books

*Ancient Greeks*, Stephanie Turnbull (Usborne Books, 2004)

*Time Travel Guide: Ancient Greece,* Anna Claybourne (Raintree Freestyle Express, 2008)

## Websites

**http://www.ancientgreece.co.uk/**
Learn about the Ancient Greeks on this British Museum website.

## Places to visit

The British Museum, London

**www.britishmuseum.org/**
Visit the Ancient Greece and Rome Gallery at the British Museum to find out more about the Ancient Greeks.

**Find out**

Name a race that the Ancient Greeks took part in.

# Index

Alexander the Great
  22–23
Amazons 25
Ancient Greek Empire 6
armour 8, 18
Athens 8

bows and arrows 18

city-states 5, 6, 16

dory 18

films 9
foot soldiers 13, 14, 18

helmets 18, 19
hoplites 13
horses 17

Medusa 7

Olympic Games 5

Perseus 7
phalanxes 14, 15, 16

Romans 5, 26

sesame buns 28–29
shields 12, 14, 15, 18
slaves 25
soldiers 12–17, 18, 20–21,
  26, 27, 28
Sparta 5, 10, 11, 24
spears 5, 14, 16, 18
stone-slingers 20–21
swords 18

training 8, 10
tunics 11

warriors 5, 7, 18, 26
warrior women 25
weapons 5, 8, 10, 14, 16,
  18
women 24–25